# Trucks

Experts on reading levels
have consulted on the text and
concepts in this book.

At the end of the book is a "Look Back and Find" section
which provides additional information and encourages
the reader to refer back to previous pages
for the answers to the questions posed.

*Published by*
Franklin Watts, 96 Leonard Street, London EC2A 4RH

Franklin Watts Australia, 14 Mars Road, Lane Cove NSW 2066

ISBN: Paperback edition 0 7496 0400 X
Hardback edition 0 86313 458 0

© 1986 Franklin Watts/Aladdin Books

Paperback edition 1990

Hardback edition published
in the First Library series

*Designed and produced by:*
Aladdin Books Ltd, 28 Percy Street, London W1P 9FF

*Printed in Belgium*

# Trucks

by
Kate Petty

Consultant
Angela Grunsell

Illustrated by
Chris Forsey

Franklin Watts
New York · London · Toronto · Sydney

Have you ever noticed all the different trucks roaring up and down the motorways, day and night? Many of them carry goods to fill the shelves of stores and supermarkets.

Ford pick-up

Trucks are built to shift enormous loads from one place to another. Truckers need a special licence to drive such a big, heavy vehicle.

AF 3600 Spacecab

Trucks are either "articulated" or "rigid". The trailer of an articulated truck is hooked on to the tractor or cab unit. A rigid truck is built in one piece.

cab-over tractor unit

Some trucks are still made with the engine in front of the cab. Most modern trucks have cab-over tractor units where the engine is underneath the cab.

rigid truck

tractor unit of articulated truck

9

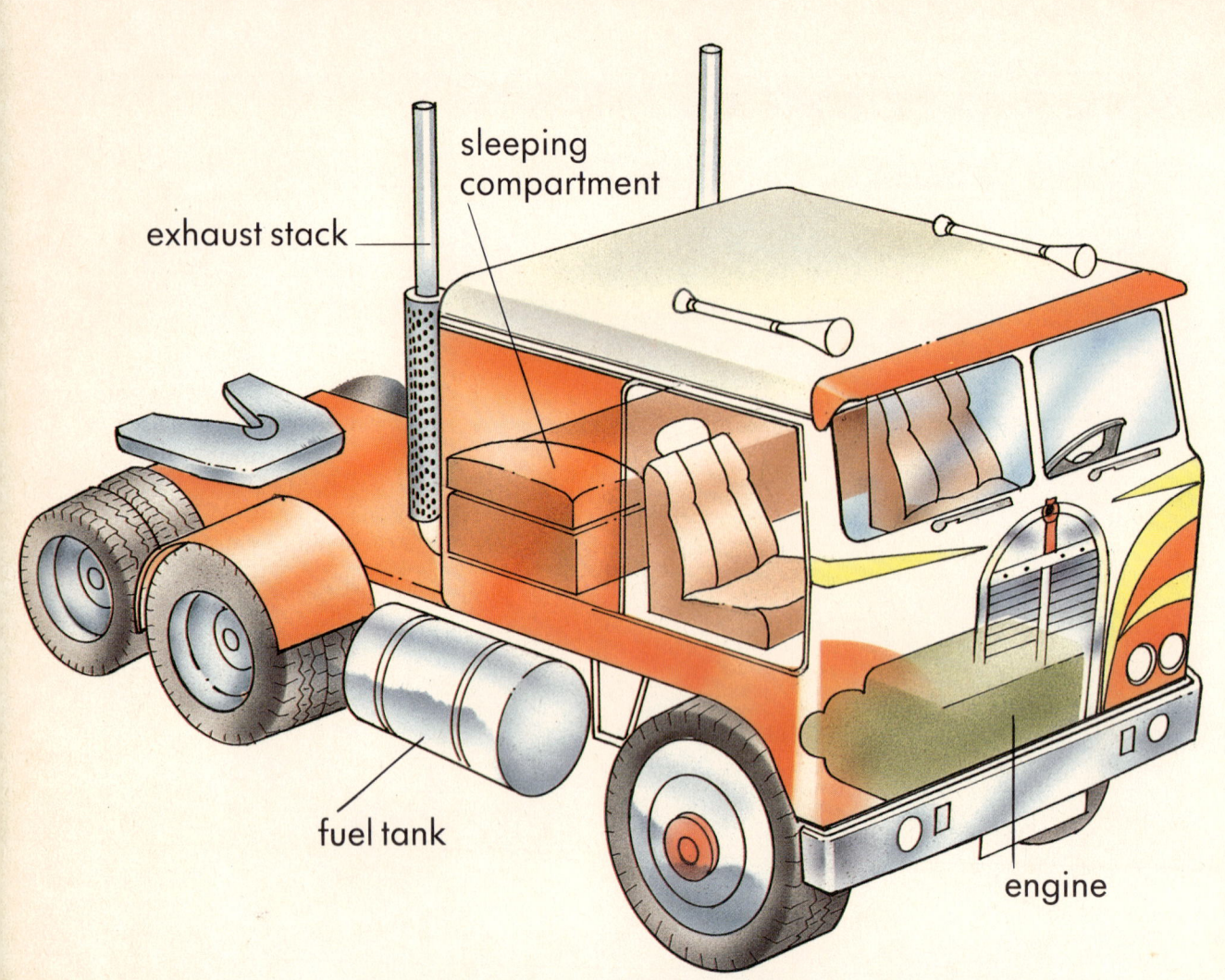

A car usually has four or five gears. Some trucks have fifteen gears or more to give them extra pulling strength. They all have powerful engines which run on diesel fuel.

10

Long-distance drivers travel for thousands of miles. They can sleep, cook and even watch TV in the cab. With CB (citizens' band) radio they can warn each other about problems ahead.

Renault contain

Many of the things you buy are brought across the sea in sealed metal boxes called containers. The containers are unloaded straight from the ship on to trucks.

Scania car transporter

New cars are driven on to car transporters. The top deck is folded down and loaded before the lower deck. The cars are held firmly in place with chains.

This Kenworth diesel truck transported the space shuttle. The shuttle weighed 75 tonnes but the 20-gear truck is able to haul loads of over 500 tonnes.

The low-loading trailer has 90 wheels. An "abnormal" load is always escorted by police cars which clear a way through the traffic.

Kenworth

This is a road train raising clouds of dust as it thunders along a dirt road in the outback of Australia. Road trains pull two or three "dog trailers" at a time.

Mack road train

They cover the long distances between towns in countries like Australia, where there are few railways. "Roo bars" on the front ward off large animals – like kangaroos.

Some truckers who own their trucks like to make them quite different from anyone else's. This is called customising.

customised Peterbilt cab

All truck drivers depend on their trucks
not to let them down in bad weather.
When it is really cold these Russian drivers
light small fires to stop the diesel oil freezing.

Terex Titan

All these trucks have a special job to do. This 30-metre logger has a hydraulic loader behind the cab for loading telegraph poles on to the trailer.

Autocar cement-mixer

Terberg tipper

You often see cement-mixers and tippers on the highways. But the Terex Titan dumper is too enormous to travel by road. The parts have to be put together on the site.

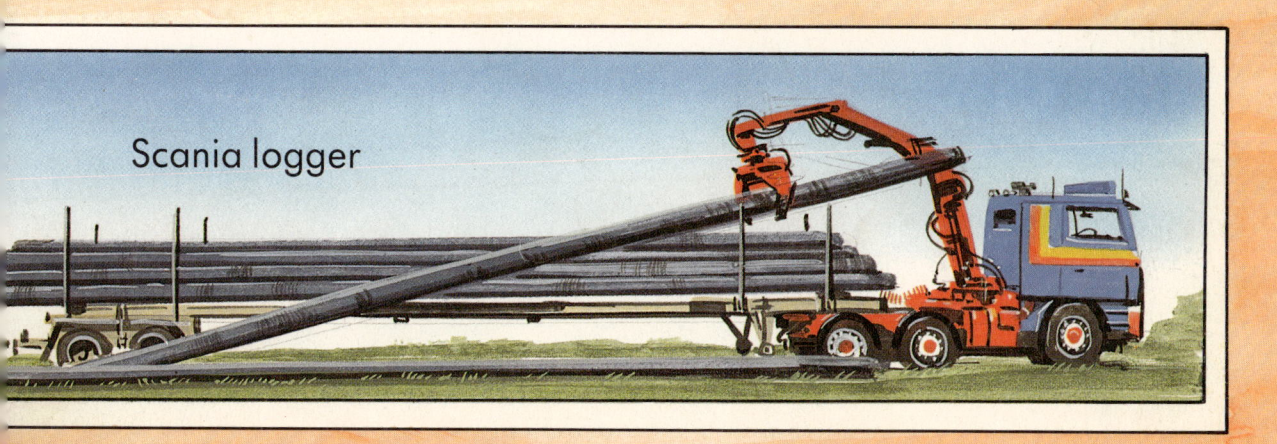

Scania logger

The New York Fire Department has 140 of these giant "tiller" fire trucks. They are 12 metres long. The ladders pull out to 30 metres so the firefighters can reach people in high buildings.

Seagrave "tiller" fire truck

There is a driver at each end of this truck. The back driver controls the rear wheels as they go round corners. Fire trucks have to reach the fire safely as well as quickly.

Atkinson petrol-tanker

Petrol is brought to the petrol station in a tanker. It is piped into tanks below the pumps. Tankers carry other liquids too – like milk and even liquid chocolate.

Kenworth breakdown truck

When a car breaks down it has to be
moved off the road.
The breakdown truck tows it
to a garage to be repaired.

Races and rallies are held for trucks as well as cars and motorbikes. This two-engined truck was specially built for the 15,000 km Paris–Dakar rally.

DAF Turbotwin rally truck

Exciting races around a circuit test the speed and road-holding of truck cabs. This truck cruises at 80 kph on the road but here it is racing at 120 kph.

Peterbilt cab unit

# Look back and find

What is this part of an articulated truck called?

Why is it easy to tell the difference between a rigid truck and an articulated one when they go round corners?

What does TIR stand for?
*Transports Internationaux Routiers.
Trucks travelling abroad with this sign are checked by Customs at the start and finish of their journey.
Then they don't need to be checked at every foreign border.*

In which countries are road trains used?
*Australia, Canada, Alaska. Desert trains in Africa have special tyres and large radiators.*

Why don't they travel on the highways?

How long can a road train be?
*Up to 45 metres.*

**How does a tipper truck tip?**
*The back end of the truck is hinged to the chassis. The front end is pushed up by a hydraulic bar.*

**What does a cement-mixer do?**
*The barrel turns to mix the concrete as the cement-mixer drives along.*

**How many drivers does this fire truck have?**

**How many firefighters are on it?**
*There are four firefighters and one officer.*

**Why do you think it is called a "tiller" truck?**

**What shape is a tanker?**

**What sorts of liquids do tankers carry?**

**What else might they carry?**

**Where has this tanker come from?**
*It has come from the oil refinery.*

# Index

| | | | |
|---|---|---|---|
| A | articulated truck 8<br>Atkinson 24<br>Autocar 21 | L | logger 20 |
| | | M | Mack 16, 17 |
| B | breakdown truck 25 | P | Paris–Dakar rally 26<br>Peterbilt 18, 27<br>pick-up 6, 7 |
| C | cab 8, 9, 11<br>cab-over tractor unit 9<br>car transporter 13<br>cement-mixer 21<br>citizens' band radio 11<br>containers 12<br>customising 18 | R | racing 26, 27<br>rally truck 26<br>Renault 12<br>rigid truck 8<br>road train 16, 17<br>roo bars 17 |
| D | DAF 6, 7<br>diesel 10, 14, 19<br>dog trailer 16 | S | Scania 13, 20<br>Seagrave 22 |
| F | fire truck 22, 23<br>Ford 6 | T | Terberg 21<br>Terex Titan 21<br>tipper 21 |
| G | gears 10, 14 | | |
| K | Kenworth 14, 25 | | |

PRINTED IN BELGIUM BY
proost
INTERNATIONAL BOOK PRODUCTION